Braveheart:
Get Your Heart Together Guide

La'Toya Hart

BRAVEHEART:
Get Your Heart Together Guide

La'Toya Hart

ISBN: 978-0-692-84594-3

Contents

INTRODUCTION

The smell and feeling of love is the most exciting experience – when you are in love you are hopeful for the future and you look forward to making life long memories with your mate. Eventually, we have to face the hard truth – a truth that may seem unfair and hard to believe. That truth is everything that looks good and feels good isn't always good for you. The reality is sometimes you can want something so bad that you attempt to fill the position with anyone having a warm heart and a pulse – without giving much consideration to whether the person really meets your requirements.

Like many women, I understand the relationship struggle. It was difficult being a single woman prior to before meeting my husband. There are really great men waiting to be blessed with a wife and there are also a tribe of phoebes and bad boys; who want nothing more than to roll around in the sheets. When you are in a relationship for the wrong reasons your heart will cry out for more and you will be filled with discontent. Like most women, I kept close count on my biological clock because I knew I wanted to have children and be a wife, but I was stuck. The desire to have a family is significant, but not worth creating a future filled with heartache and grief.

By the age of twenty-five, I was experiencing my third and worst breakup ever. It didn't matter what I did or how hard I tried to get over my broken heart, nothing seemed to work. I was so heart broken I even thought about going back several times because I wanted my happily ever after. We spent almost ten years together; we were entitled to spend a lifetime together. However, I knew I couldn't go back because things were irreparably broken – so I had to move on. It was time for me to find peace with the relationship and heal my heart.

I began my journey to healing while attending Wilmington University. College gave me an opportunity to take classes, which in turn allowed me to learn the keys to healing from my breakup. I get it, you might be thinking going to college was such a bold move, but I wanted to move forward and I didn't have anyone to help me on my journey. By the way, I do not encourage you to follow my approach – it cost me thousands of dollars and it took years.

Once I healed my own heart I began sharing my secret of success with other women and a movement started. A movement of women empowered to love on their own terms. Thousands of women around the world have attended my virtual conferences and achieved extraordinary results; reclaiming joy, peace, and personal power.

Braveheart is about the action required to heal your heart. It is about choosing to keep pushing even when you are consumed with the desire to withdraw. Braveheart will teach you how to kick your inner critic and allow you to tap into your inner super woman - showing the world just how Brave, Bold, and Powerful you are.

Living a fulfilling and happy life is up to you. The best way to get over an old love is to fall in love with *you* and continue to work on loving *yourself.* If you haven't already done so, IT IS TIME! This book will give you the tools to attract love and live the life you deserve.

CHAPTER ONE
Why the Breakup
Came Without Warning

Your 'significant other' has initiated a conversation concerning the relationship by uttering the dreaded words, "We need to talk." "This is the end," your mind screams. You desperately wish for it to be just one of those "other talks" despite the reality that the relationship hasn't been as great as it was during the first few months.

You can feel that pit forming in your stomach as you reminisce about the good times you shared with him. Reflecting on those moments when he had been very supportive despite your constant fights and moments of pure madness that have led up to this moment.

In a matter of minutes, the relationship is over.

Months or years of building trust have now gone down the drain. Worse still, the breakup came without any prior warning and this seems to amplify the difficulty for the partner that was let go.

Whichever way, the situation applies to all of us, we must all understand and accept the reality that all romantic relationships are not meant to naturally end with a walk down the aisle; no matter how intense the efforts were by the parties involved. However, as human beings, it is expected that we be prepared to move on from any bad situation life may bring. There is no point beating yourself up and allowing your emotions to be immersed in self-guilt. Healing and moving on is definitely not an easy task, but it is one we can come out on top of, if we are bold enough to take on the journey.

There are a few important ways to get past the initial shock of a split and right choices that will make you feel invincible and confident about reclaiming joy as a single. Wrong decisions, however, will have you spending many days lying in bed with feelings of depression, replaying memories of the relationship in your mind, and wondering what went wrong.

If you are reading this, it is probably safe to assume you've been through a breakup and one of the first things you probably did was cry. Naturally, thoughts of pleading with him to come back probably crossed your mind too. This is a perfectly natural, human response to relationship disasters and it originates from our fear of the future.

"What will tomorrow bring? Isn't it better to stick with the devil I know, instead of meeting someone new that might be worse than him?" Most ladies ask these questions and are tempted to go back to their previous relationship with little hope of changing the former lover.

Many years ago, I cried my eyes out after a breakup. I even questioned my decision to leave because the pain seemed too much for me to endure. The instant gratification of going back and moving away from the agony seemed like a better option at the time. Even though it was a known fact that my ex was a serial-cheater who could not keep his eyes off other girls, I still entertained the idea of going back to put up with his childish ways and continue praying he might change. Well, it's a good thing those thoughts did not become reality, because I would have wasted my time trying to salvage a relationship my boyfriend was content in breaking down through his indiscipline and non-commitment.

The first step to healing is to recognize and accept that there is a better future ahead and life is preparing you for it, even though you may get hurt in the process. The reason for this long journey filled with bumps and bruises is to BUILD you into a strong woman capable of handling pressure, overcoming foes, and trusting in God at every turn.

After all, our hearts belong to God; He is the only one who can truly change us. Though it may sound absurd, we might have to experience heartbreak before coming to realize this fact. We should be grateful that we did not take the big leap into marriage before realizing the harsh reality that no matter how much effort put into trying to fix a man; only God can change the heart.

Some women think that jumping into another relationship with someone else will make the hurt go away, but the possibility of the hurt leaving, is almost non-existent. After a breakup, you must learn to look within to understand and define your priorities. Breakups are the perfect time to explore your new individual identity through self-exploration. During self-exploration you must let pent up emotions flow. Surround yourself with family and close friends who will be your support team.

With the help of your loved ones, the feeling of loneliness will subside as they cheer you up and encourage you. Their presence will serve as a reminder that there are other important, meaningful people in your life. Remember that life is not only meant to be enjoyed within the confines of a romantic relationship, but also in the company of friends and family. Some people choose to deal with heartbreak by staying alone; I believe it is far more beneficial to be surrounded by people who love and care about you.

For those people who choose to put on a strong front and keep their emotions bottled up, remember there are no prizes to be won for being tough. It does more harm than good when we put up a wall to cover our hurt. For some people, the hurt becomes a part of their character, they become conditioned to think and act according to that pattern of thought.

For example, have you ever wondered why some women have the fixed notion that ALL MEN CHEAT? I know you must have heard this statement being used at some point.

In most cases, women who subscribe to this notion have not healed completely from a previous relationship and allow themselves to judge their new partners based on the characteristics of the former person who hurt them. Without getting to know the unique personality of the new guy, they unknowingly refuse to build trust in him and that lack of trust is the number one killer of relationships.

There are no two fingerprints alike and no two people are the same. Because of our different upbringings and knowledge garnered over the years, we possess different values and character traits. If you refuse to heal from the past this may cause you to develop an unhealthy approach towards relationships with men both in formal circles like your workplace and informal settings like a romantic relationship.

If you know women who have preconceived notions of how members of the opposite sex act, know that it may be a result of their inability to move on from past hurt. They keep carrying the old baggage that causes them to be blind to the benefits they could enjoy if they could just trust their new partners - a trust that ushers in peaceful living and true love without fear.

Now that you are finished venting your emotions as part of the healing process, it is time to embrace a new and improved you. This is the perfect time to enjoy the benefits of being single again. You can do this by pronouncing a small phrase, "I am now Single."

Notice, I didn't say, "Now I am alone." This is because singleness belongs to you but you do not belong to it. You are not defined by it. This is your time of refreshing and rebooting your life. It is a time to love you without having to please other people or fit into their description of a perfect person. Enjoy a walk with friends, take yourself out and engage in crazy stuff that will bring your groove back.

Most people incorrectly believe that being single is a curse; they fail to enjoy its inherent benefits. You can enroll in self- development courses or engage in charitable volunteer activities in your neighborhood. From these activities, you can derive pure joy without any feelings of guilt or fear of hurting anyone. Being single also means that you have opportunities to build a greater network of friends of the opposite sex. This may have been restricted in your previous relationship because male partners may get jealous when their girlfriends spend time with male friends or coworkers. Being single, there is no one to feel jealous about your relationships; this paves the way for you to enjoy being around other friends.

At this time, you can learn more about them while not feeling the pressure to commit to a romantic relationship.

It is very important that you build a closer relationship with your friends and family. Families are indispensable on the road to recovery for anybody and the more you get to be with them, the more you feel secure. This security is a great boost for morale and also ensures that you are able to overcome or avoid an inferiority complex, the feeling that you are not good enough. Once you have the confidence that you are loved and important to family, you will be less eager to jump into the arms of anyone who comes along offering a romantic relationship. Strengthening family bonds also means it will be easier to overcome future heartbreak and disappointment.

Remember I mentioned the fact that there is a greater plan for your life? Well, it is important that you key into your purpose. Knowing that God loves you with an unbridled love and calls you the apple of His eye, you should desire to know Him during this period of hurt and rediscovery.

I want you to know the road to getting your groove back is not going to be an easy one but it is one that will mold you into a better person who will enjoy future relationships without hurt.

CHAPTER TWO
Why People Fall Out of Love

Though we all enter romantic relationships with the hope and mindset that the bond and love shared will last forever, some relationships do fall by the wayside for varying reasons. Why does love fade or grow cold replacing a once blazing fire of romance? What are the most common activities or habits that one partner develops completely freaking out the other partner or causing them to lose interest? Well, hang on tight as we delve into these issues of the heart.

It is common knowledge that a relationship can be going fine then suddenly it begins to decline and a short time later, it's over. As human beings, some people fall out of love because they all have an inherent desire to achieve complete satisfaction. These folks typically enter relationships with an unrealistic picture of what they hope to gain. As the relationship progresses they discover a reality, which is much different than they pictured, leading to feelings of dissatisfaction with the relationship.

Take for example the case of a guy who enters a relationship with the major aim to satisfy his sexual hunger. This is the number one reason why most men initiate relationship moves and the number one reason why those relationships die out. Lust is often mistaken for love because it is such a powerful force. Two people can easily become engulfed in an undeniably, intense, physical attraction; especially of a sexual nature. An example of lust is what a man might feel when he sees an extremely attractive woman. At that moment, he is only attracted to the physical features of the lady. She may have a pretty face, causing most men to drool or thick thighs that drive men crazy. Because a woman consists of much more than her physical appearance, this relationship is starting off on the wrong foot. Later, when the man discovers that she has flaws, discontent enters. He may becomes tired of seeing her face without makeup and become distracted when he sees another lady with a prettier face and appealing curves and features, he moves on quickly.

Lust is very different from love. When you are in love with someone, you see a future with them, you take an interest in their core values, and they are included in your life plans. Lust on the other hand is typically a short-term infatuation. Sometimes it can be difficult to determine the difference between love and infatuation – both can cause powerful feelings. The key thing to remember about love is – it doesn't only bring people together but it keeps people together long after the initial fire of a relationship has faded. Love is having a deep affection for someone that lasts the test of time. Unfortunately, once the fire dies down, one or both people begin to realize what the relationship is lacking and can begin to desire a relationship with more depth.

This same theory can be applicable to ladies who go into relationships with a wrong mindset and end up with regrets. Some may fall in love with a guy because of his great abs and physique while others love rich guys who can spoil them. Giving is part of love, as a matter of fact; giving is the language of love. Exchanging gifts is part of every true relationship but giving does not necessarily mean love - neither is it a true measure of love. However, it is wrong to go into a relationship with someone simply because of the financial and material capacity of the other person. Go into a relationship because of love. A relationship that is built on anything other than love is a relationship that has been set up to fail. I can assure you that money can buy a lot of things in life but there are some things that are above the purchasing power of money and two of those are love and happiness. If you marry a person because he or she is rich, you may eventually become unhappy in the marriage and money would not be much help.

Remember Tyler Perry's film 'Marriage Counselor' in which the wife of a local pharmacist fell in love with a rich young mogul. Though their illicit relationship was passionate for a while (making love in private jets and multimillion dollar mansions), the guy turned abusive and later infected her with AIDS.

With that example and many more that we witness in real life experiences, it is very important that we approach every relationship with the right mindset. We have to love someone for who they truly are on the inside and not just physical attraction or what they own in terms of wealth.

Here are some signs that the love was NOT authentic:

- There is an intense cravings to satisfy sexual hunger.

- The relationship is demanding and impulsive in nature.

- There is a desire to be with them only for what they can offer.

- There is more fire and very little stability.

- You are more focused on their outside appearance than what's on the inside.

- You experience intense neediness and seek to control and manipulate.

- The feeling of lust is conditional and will only survive if you get what you want.

Another major problem that leads to broken relationships is impatience. Impatience is the unwillingness to let time have its place in building your bond.

Have you ever heard the phrase, "Rome was not built in a day?" Well, relationships too are not built in a day. Sadly, some people seem to possess an insane belief that if their partners don't change within a certain number of days, they will never change. This line of thinking brings dissatisfaction and creates a barrier between lovers, which can ultimately degenerate into divorce for married couples, or a break up in unmarried partners.

It's important to understand the reality that nothing good comes easy and if you want your relationship to be perfect, you must be willing to give it time. Since partners come from different backgrounds, it is perfectly normal that some of their interests and characteristics may be irritating to one another. The guy may always leave the toilet seat up while the girl may be a fashion addict. The guy may be addicted to smoking while the girl may love hanging out with friends. I could go further but you get the point that we all differ. No two people are exactly the same; therefore the way we perceive things differs one from another. Give yourself time to understand the peculiarities in your partner's behavior. Trust me, with time you two will understand each other better and be able to recognize positive traits and qualities in each other.

Because we all strive for excellence, we may want to try and force our partners to fit into our perfect image of a partner and this process can be frustrating. However, we can help them become better if we adopt a patient and gentle approach. Since no one likes being ordered around like a servant, partners in a relationship must be respectful towards each other at all times. Mutual respect is like oil and lubrication to the engine of love, it simply keeps it working smoothly.

Communication is a key part of all relationships. In formal settings, communication fosters mutual understanding and fulfillment of goals while in informal settings, like a romantic bond, it is similar to dancing with your man. With great practice, you are able to catch your partner's rhythm and things flow effortlessly. Most importantly, when the beat changes you are able to realign your moves to fit your partner's. When you aren't able to pick up your partners rhythm things gradually decline. Similar to dancing, communication requires both parties to be able to talk at all times and that is why you are in a relationship. You are each other's confidant. You must be able to find a way to share your feelings and re-align with your already set goals.

For most women, this role is easy to play while the reverse is usually the case for most men. It is your responsibility as a woman to encourage your man to listen and learn to share. This action, however, must not be accomplished through threats or force (no one likes being controlled), but through gentle persuasion and respect. Endeavor to patiently explain why communication is important to you.

Deborah Tannen, a professor of sociolinguistics at Georgetown University wrote a book highlighting her research on men and women's differing communication styles. (Tannan, 2007) Tannen's research showed that most men do not understand the importance of communication with their partners. Hence, they are always downright bewildered and confused when their female partners pick a fight over their lack of communication. Like I stated earlier, you must patiently guide and teach him how the female mind works. Remind him that while he may be fine with a short chat, you desire a longer, more intimate talk.

When both parties in a relationship are not dancing to the same tune it creates a breakdown in communication. Communication problems leave a backlog of unresolved issues, which could eventually metamorphose into resentment and anger. Couples drift apart when one or both are left unheard, emotions aren't expressed or they are just not on the same page anymore. Don't just communicate alone; also endeavor to pay attention to what your partner is saying because doing this increases their sense of value, relevance and worth in the relationship.

Allowing conflicts to pile up instead of addressing them can lead to couples drifting apart. When disagreements remain unresolved things can get worse. The couple's connection and love is lost and ultimately a split can occur. Regular conflict and tension create an unhealthy dynamic. It makes the relationship uncomfortable, stressful, and naturally, one or both partners will eventually look for an escape.

To put this knowledge into a better context, ABC news conducted a poll across the USA in 2003 discovering that ninety-six percent of couples polled, listed communication as the number one factor that sustains their marriage. Because of effective communication, their union grew by leaps and bounds and many were able to survive the divorce scare.

Taking each other for granted is another common cause of breakups. We can all remember the feeling we experienced when we fell in love. We could not do without hearing our partners voice for ten minutes after leaving them. We rushed home to cuddle while eating popcorn and watching Netflix. We adored their very presence and longed to smell their cologne. Then, it started fading away. We started losing interest in seeing them and they became just another roommate. We become more comfortable wearing no makeup and leaving the dishes unwashed and our man allows his beard to regrow without paying attention to personal grooming. We reach the point where we both get too used to each other. Complacency is a silent killer of relationships. It stifles the passion.

Another damaging stage in relationships comes when one party keeps giving without getting anything in return or respect goes away because both think the other person will always be there. This may go unnoticed for some time, but it breeds discontent, sometimes hatred, for each other. When they both stop appreciating one another, stop respecting their individual choices, and begin feeling indifferent to each other's concerns, problems start to come and it may ultimately lead to divorce.

I have a female friend who confided in me. She was already tired of her relationship, had already met someone new and was looking for a way to call it quits. It turns out her present partner had stopped paying her compliments or giving her the attention her heart craved. The new guy, on the other hand, was respectful, charming and made her feel wanted. He proclaimed her "queen of his world" and was always sending gifts as evidence of his feelings. Although she had initially rejected him, she began to love him following his consistent compliments and his willingness to provide a listening ear to her problems. If complements were a major part of the blossoming stages of your relationship, you should continue it as the months and years go by.

It is very important that you continue to respect each other and appreciate each other. It is up to you to make sure that you fan the fire of your love by spicing up your relationship at all times. Do not be stuck doing the same thing, spice up your love life by doing crazy things every once in a while. Remember to renew your vows of love to each other while making sure that you provide listening ears to help your partner battle through challenges he may be enduring or vice versa.

A solid foundation of any relationship must be composed of common values, interests, good communication, and strong conflict resolution skills. A single missing component creates weak spots that can ultimately become deal breakers. Common values are crucial because they reduce instances of conflict. A similar interest builds the friendship portion of a healthy romance and great communication limits the risk of expressing yourself. Conflict resolution means having the ability to respect differences and encourage compromise. What this means is that in the event of a disagreement, for the sake of peace and quick resolution, either of the two parties or both will have to be flexible and compromise.

Relationships are always amazing at the beginning because of the newness associated with a fresh romance. At the beginning of a relationship you truly understand the statement "Love is a beautiful thing." During the initial phase, two individuals are just getting to know one another. All exchanges are interesting, witty, and you paint yourself and each other in a positive light. As time passes, layers are peeled back. The problem comes when you discover things about your partner that are unsatisfactory, if not intolerable. We'll call them non-negotiable. Upon those discoveries, a breakup can happen because they force you to realize that the relationship isn't a good fit. Sometimes two people just aren't meant to be.

Before entering a relationship you must perform a self-assessment. You must ask yourself very important questions, such as, "Do I really love the person I am going to be in a relationship with or am I looking for a quick fix to boost my mood? Am I really interested in this person? Would I be proud to introduce this person as my partner? Do I really want to be in a relationship at this time, etc.?" The genuine answers to these questions will determine whether you are truly ready.

CHAPTER THREE
7 Phases of the Breakup Process

We spend most of our lives building relationships and we continue to do this until the day we breathe our last breath. Our first relationship is with parents/guardians and siblings before subsequently branching out to non-family members as we continue to grow. As a matter of fact, every activity we engage in on a daily basis is all about building and sustaining relationships with those around us.

We can say, a relationship is like a house built from scratch, while a break up is like demolishing the house that has taken years or months to build (depending on the duration of the relationship). The joy of being in a happy relationship is one that is difficult to describe. It gives you a deep sense comfort and a thrill very few activities or endeavors can.

However sweet the feelings of being in a relationship can be, the reality is that not all relationships last, indeed, quite a lot end in breakups.

Breakups are not a trivial matter. To some, it is just a case of moving on and looking ahead, while to others, it is much more complex. It can affect the attitudes and behaviors of those involved and lead to a total breakdown in some instances. It can lead to addictions as well as substance abuse.

Have you ever had a cut, perhaps from a household or sporting incident and you had to yank off a part of the skin atop the wound so you could apply first aid and subsequently seek further treatment? I am sure the procedure was painful! Why? Because it involves removing a part of your skin! That is comparable to what happens during a break up. It is like shredding a part of you and removing it.

There are different stages to a break up. From how you process the initial news to ultimately moving on. Although avoidance is the easiest route to take in order to quickly escape and forget the pain, it is better to go through all the seven stages of healing after a break up. This ensures that you can both handle the situation with dignity and without harboring ill will that may cause your future relationships to crumble. Knowing how to deal with a breakup is truly important; it is useful for you and for those around you who may be experiencing a break up.

Please note that these are the initial stages and

working through any pain left behind is a whole new process.

We will go through all the seven stages of the breakup process and include tips on how to get through each one successfully.

SHOCK

"Hey, I don't think this relationship can work out. I can't go on like this"

When you hear these words from your man, your initial and natural reaction is shock. Even though you may have known the relationship is on the rocks and on the verge of a break up, that statement will still catch you by surprise. Depending on the state of the relationship prior to the break up, the level of shock may vary. If the relationship has been off and on or has been showing signs of weakening there's still a sense of shock that will come from the announcement of a breakup. Once the words are spoken it effectively puts the final nail in the coffin. Any hope you might have about the possibility of a resolution is gone. Even more profound is the feeling of emotional shock that could arise from the announcement of a break up suddenly, out of the blue.

Everyone responds differently to a break up. Some may immediately burst into tears while others may want to sit down and have a heart to heart dialogue. There are instances where tears can turn to rage or anger; this can result in damaging or destroying valuable things while in a blind fit of anger. Still, others become overwhelmingly ill or develop mental issues. How you respond to the news is very impactful. As women, we tend to be emotional beings and one of the most precise emotional triggers is a breakup because tons of time and emotions have been invested in building the relationship, therefore, its collapse will trigger a surge of emotions of which shock is dominant.

During this stage, you may have no idea why this is happening to you. You are overwhelmed with either rage or tears, by the impact of losing someone you care about.

You begin to realize that they are not going to be part of your life anymore and your thoughts become cluttered with thoughts of rejection, worthlessness, and a overabundance of other degrading thoughts. Shock, sometimes, causes a lack of understanding for what is happening in the moment, his makes the situation worse because you can fall into a deep sea of denial.

DENIAL

Once, I mentored a woman whose friends had insisted that she meet with me. Her friends told me her romantic relationship had just ended; yet she acted like she was still in a relationship with the guy. When I started engaging in discussion with her, her first reaction was to deny that her relationship had ended. Turns out, she had a deep bond with the guy and could not bring herself to wake up to the reality that he had called it quits. She had continued to call him at odd hours like couples do and eventually went to his apartment uninvited. Worse still, she scared off a potential girlfriend.

This is an example of the denial stage, also known as the stage when breakups get quite problematic. When one individual cannot accept that the relationship is over they may say to themselves, "This is a temporary break, we'll find our way back to each other." Maybe they take it a step further by continually pursing the relationship. Living in denial over a long period of time can be very damaging for the personality of the person involved because they have a detachment from what is really happening. In some cases psychological disorders can be tied to this type of denial.

You don't want this to be you because

1. It isn't healthy
2. This is how stalking starts.

To overcome denial, you have to understand it. A person likely feels compelled to seek anything remotely close to the relationship. This is often done through texting, calling or Facebook stalking because it is better than the truth and the hurt that truth brings. Instead of sticking with the above activities, you must find time to engage in talking with family and friends. At this point, it is also very necessary to visit a counselor or a psychologist who can help you come to grips with reality. This is not an easy process at all but with the help of loved ones, you will be able to overcome it and prevent yourself from engaging in activities that may damage your reputation or the safety of your previous romantic partner. In this world of increased social media awareness, there are online support groups where you can join others to be encouraged by women and their journey.

Desperate For Answers

Let me tell you now, each stage may not happen consecutively. However, they are the most common stages experienced after a break up. During this stage of a breakup, most women are desperate for answers. This is a direct result of coming to terms with the reality of your loss. Some women will politely demand a sit down, heart to heart talk.

Here are some of the questions racing through the minds of most newly single women:

1. What went wrong?

   You want to know what brought you to the point of no return.

2. How did this happen?

   You want to know what fueled the decision

to finally call it quits without trying other means of resolving conflicts.

3. What did I do?

Because guilt tends to build up in the heart, you want to know where you went wrong. You think if you figure out what happened you can apologize or work on improving to make your next relationship better.

4. Is there someone else?

This tends to be one of the questions most women ask after a break up. They may have the impression they are no longer desirable. In some cases, women end up changing who they are authentically in an effort to win over the ex-boyfriend. The problem with this is that you likely aren't ready to hear the truth, let alone process it. The driving force for wanting to know what happened at this point – is wanting to know the reason behind the breakup so you can persuade your ex to work things out.

The time to get these questions answered is when most of the pain is behind you and you just want closure to fully move on. Once you reach the point when you're ready to move on, you might not even want those questions answered.

BARGAINING

This is the stage when things can get a little desperate, but no worries, because it is all part of the process. Bargaining is basically negotiating with yourself, your ex and your future happiness. There are two reasons behind bargaining. One is just trying to get your ex back (most long for a second chance) while the other is an attempt to free yourself of guilt because you think a specific event or set of events you caused has led to the split. Such bargaining may include vows to never make the same mistakes again, extreme measures like making deals with your ex to change something about yourself (like your physical appearance or personality). You may even end up promising yourself, family, and friends that you will be a better person. Though bargaining may work sometimes, it may be very unhealthy for you because by placing all the blame on yourself, you start developing a shield mentality that forces you to protect others before protecting yourself.

What do I mean?

Some women take ownership for everything that went wrong in the relationship. They release their man of any blame and continue to psychologically beat themselves up over the mistakes they made. You may know a mother who never corrects their child because they fear the child will be harmed emotionally. Over time, the child feels invincible and eventually causes the mother undue stress and emotional pain. The worst part is the mother still continues to blame herself for their actions.

Please keep in mind that both people in a relationship contributed to the end of the connection and the blame must be shared. This means that in order for the relationship to get back on track, BOTH people must agree to change something about them to make it work.

RELAPSE

There are some times where your efforts to get back together can be successful. The problem is that the reconciliation may not be for the right reasons. Yes, couples that stand the test of time have broken up, gotten back together again and were stronger than ever.

After a breakup, some women have a fear of being alone. They don't want to date again, they wonder what life will be like without their man, and they're scared of the pain, the sadness, the adjustment, and the unknown. This is when you have to decode whether the willingness to try again is genuine or simply a way to escape the pain of a break up.

ANGER

This emotion leaves you feeling pissed anytime you think of your ex or actually see him in person. For some women, anger accompanies the feeling of rejection while others are angry because of the number of years and resources they spent trying to make the relationship work. Make no mistake, there is nothing wrong with being angry but you must monitor your emotions to exercise caution and restraint in the way you express them. Destructive outbursts of rage will not make you feel better. Breaking things is definitely not going to repair the broken union; rather it portrays you as being mentally unstable.

You can deal with the anger by doing the following:

1. Talking about it.

2. Journaling about it.

3. Getting it out through physical activities such as boxing, running and so much more.

Spreading nasty rumors, keying cars, bleaching clothes, holding belongings hostage and blackmailing are all reactions that may get you in trouble. Anger is a tricky thing. When you are furious, acting on the angry thoughts seems like the only way to get relief. This is why they say, "Misery loves company." You're mad so you want to spread the ill feelings around to make yourself feel better. However, doing so is a sad attempt to fulfill your desire to place blame. Think before you act and ask yourself, "What is this really going to achieve?" Like I have mentioned previously, and will continue to stress, get the support of your loved ones. This will help you redirect your feelings of anger and your need for companionship.

ACCEPTANCE

This is the final stage that represents progress. Even though the pain remains and there is a healing process ahead, I urge you to look on the bright side. The fact that you are not stuck in the denial stage represents a big leap and indicates a readiness to move on and enjoy life. Now you will be able to engage in self-analysis and re-evaluation of future relationship goals. Understanding comes with acceptance. You understand why you fell for your ex in the first place, are able to identify what went wrong in the relationship, and there is a level of peace achieved. Although the weight isn't completely off your shoulders, there is a sense of relief that comes with acceptance. You now have a sense of relief that brings a fresh perspective and vibrancy.

CHAPTER FOUR
How to Fall Out of Love Fast and Heal Your Heart

Many find this unbelievable but breakups impact you both mentally and physically. The body fires off pain signals that affect both the mind and body making it even more important to get it under control. Pain's effect on the mind can range from sadness and anguish to depression. These effects can cause a switch from healthy behaviors to unhealthy ones, cause irrational behavior, decrease mood, and spark something in the brain very similar to addiction. When in love, the brain is flooded with dopamine, the feel good hormone. When that is lost, you continue to crave the "high" love once provided and that craving can cause you to do things you normally wouldn't. As for the physical impact, emotional pain activates the same receptors in the brain that are activated when you are physically hurt. This can cause muscle discomfort, tightness, chest aches and numerous other forms of physical discomfort. A greater physical impact can be by the stress hormones released. Stress caused by a breakup can also aggravate the skin and cause digestive problems.

This sounds counterintuitive but you have to feel the pain to contain and ultimately get over it. After a breakup, people try too hard to avoid what they are feeling in an attempt to get on with their life, only to run to that pain later. I get it, a broken heart is one of the most difficult things you will ever experience in life, and it is so tempting to do something to distract yourself from the pain. I've seen countless women connect with a new love, to get over an old love, only to find themselves faced with a similar situation with another person, months down the road. The problem with dating someone new before you have completely mended from an old love is you haven't had time to heal and chances are you'll began the relationship for all of the wrong reasons, and it will not last. You need time to grieve in order to truly move on and sort through your thoughts. Take time for yourself to think, be sad, mad, and an overall emotional wreck. Just "you time" to discover a fresh perspective and release emotions in the comfort and privacy of your own home, but do not stay in this state too long. During this time, take care of yourself. Get plenty of rest and eat right. Both will help you get to a better space and get you on the road to healing mentally and physically. Most important, do not forget to laugh. Laughter has a magical way of gluing the pieces of a broken heart back together. As time progresses, you will feel so much better.

As previously discussed, you must accept that you are breaking up AND THEN you have to accept that it is over. To find peace in ending a relationship, focus on easing the transition from being in a relationship to being single. The first thing you want to do is avoid texting or calling your ex. During the acceptance phase, you will have to remind yourself several times that the relationship is done and staying in contact will only get your wires crossed. When you are in a relationship you develop a bond with your man. Once the relationship is over, it will take a great deal of time to untie your connection. Both you and he will find it difficult and even uncomfortable to attempt to work through the healing process while attempting to establish a friendship. Yes, you can establish boundaries and set expectations; however, with a new breakup the lines defined will be crossed and it will lead to hurt feelings, upset, and disappointment. The first order of business will be to return any of your ex's belongings. Just put the items in a box, tape it up and send it to their home. Reminders lying around the house will not do any good. Additionally, focus on identifying negative thought patterns. Acceptance is often plagued by thoughts riddled with regret or bitterness that can cause you to backslide. Learn what triggers these thoughts and do things to reduce or eliminate them. These feelings may start when you are by yourself with nothing to do, they can be triggered by a song, or for no apparent reason at all. Your best course of action is to identify the things or activities that take you back to those times in the past and find ways to reduce the triggers. Let's say a certain song triggers you to cry because it reminds you of a time you had a argument with your ex; you can prevent this trigger by listening to music streams that allow you to control what songs are played. Lastly, and most importantly, remind yourself why the relationship ended. Even though you didn't want it to, you weren't blind to the issues present. No one is. Once you get a feel for your new life, you will really be able to put the relationship behind you for good.

This is the part that will inject new life into your spirit. That romance was only a portion of your life and you have so much more to enjoy! Get out there and start living for you and only you. Chances are, friends and family were there for you right after the split and you had them to turn to for support. That is awesome, and you should be very thankful. Now it is time to lean on yourself to improve your quality of life and assert your independence.

One way to assert your independence is throwing yourself into work as long as this is a healthy outlet, meaning you are passionate about what you do.

Establishing yourself in your field and building your success is an excellent way to establish and embrace your independence. Other healthy outlets that will help you embrace your independence are reclaiming your time. Let's face it, when you are in a relationship, having time alone rarely happens. Now it is the time to celebrate being single! Who better to do that with than your close friends? They were there through the bad and now they can be there for the good. Since the tough parts of the breakup are behind you, you're pretty much over it and are enjoying life again, enjoy it even more by holding a celebration. There are a number of ways you can do this depending on your personality. You can hold a low key and casual celebration like pajamas, movies, takeout, and wine, plan an elegant party at your home, go with a livelier event at one of your favorite places to go, or go all out and plan a wild weekend in Cabo, Vegas, or Atlantic City! What are you celebrating? Well, there is freedom, being out of a situation that you know deep down wasn't right for you, embracing the fact that the universe has more interesting plans for you, and your independence! You want to celebrate because although you were hurt, you fought the negativity and managed to thrive, grow, and learn. For this celebration, make sure everyone knows why they are there and make the event lively no matter what. This isn't a pity party. Have music playing in the background, activities, games, tons of food, and the best company you know. If you aren't great at throwing celebrations, ask a friend to help or head over to Pinterest for some inspiration. When combined, the simplest things can make a memorable party.

An independence exercise you really want to try is having dinner alone. I get it, sitting at a restaurant alone doesn't seem like the ideal situation, but the best way to get to know you, and what you like/dislike is to spend more time with you. Having the courage to walk into a restaurant, utter the words, "table for one," and sit and eat your meal is empowering. A woman learns to appreciate her own company, embrace some solitude, unwind, and as a major plus, you get to eat minus the small talk! Many are hesitant at first, they feel like they are going to look lonely, fear that the whole situation will be awkward or think that other people will be looking at them in judgment. Well, one, you are not the first person to eat by themselves and you won't be the last. People dine solo all the time. Two, the only way eating alone will be awkward is if you make it awkward. Finally, no one is going to be watching you because you're alone. They are at the establishment to eat a nice meal, just like you.

The final step of embracing your independence is planning for the future. As I said, you have a lot of life ahead of you to live to the fullest so make plans for you and only you. Use the breakup as motivation to reassess your life and decide where you're going. Oftentimes, we make the mistake of thinking that a partner is always going to be there. It is easy to get wrapped up in the love and passion. As a result, we fail to make plans for ourselves. That approach isn't realistic. Breakups happen so you have to take care of yourself first and adapt our plans later if you do find "the one." Whether you have made future plans or not, create a detailed path for yourself now. Consider where you want to be in five years, set financial goals, career goals, vacation goals and any others that matter to YOU. Don't just write down what you want to achieve, make them SMART. This means they're specific, measurable, achievable, realistic, and time bound.

CHAPTER FIVE
What to do about Social Media

Why social media? You may ask, "How can social media have anything to do with the process of moving on?" Social networks play a huge role in shaping our personal and work lives and will continue to play a much deeper role as the years proceed. These networks have helped us in many ways but may also inhibit the process of moving on after a break up. An example of this would be after you've just broken up with your man, you go on Facebook to announce it. You friends send tons of virtual love support; this helps in boosting you self-esteem. You will probably receive a number of negative comments, which may be damaging to how you feel. Let's face it social media trolls are real and they are increasing at an alarming rate.

Most important, you will have a meltdown if you

see pictures of him. Even worse would be coming across a picture of him with a new love interest. It is just like leaving a sore to heal for an hour, then ripping off the bandages the next minute. If you want to heal your broken heart, you must be very diligent in how you proceed. The first thing you must do today is open your social media account and un-friend your ex. There are several reasons why un-friending is a must. First, you must detach from him and this will require you to cut off all communication for a while as you heal and get over the relationship. Social media makes contact too easy and you may feel the urge to get in touch.

Hitting the un-follow button is a must because you may feel the urge to snoop and compare your present emotional state with his. Most people go online to check out what their ex has been up to. They want to know whom he's dating, where he's been hanging out, or if he's having a difficult time moving on. True, you sometimes find comfort when you see that he is not doing so well, and does not have a new girlfriend, but what happens when you see that he is doing great and has a new girlfriend and they are posting pictures snuggling? The answer is that a certain amount of bitterness wells up in your chest. This bitterness will hinder your progress and may ultimately lead you to doing something illegal. Trust me, you are better off not knowing what is going on in their life. Focus on you and only you at this point.

Cyber stalking is not beneficial in any situation and can lead to the development of unhealthy patterns. One additional problem it may cause is that you may intentionally find yourself comparing yourself to others. One of the most common things women tell themselves after a break up is "I am not as good as his new girlfriend." This pattern of thinking breeds an inferiority complex that will drag you down in every area of your life because you will always feel someone is better.

Unfortunately, we live in an age where people let the number of social media 'likes', determine how important or beautiful they are without realizing that true beauty comes from within and cannot be determined by the size of their body features, or the amount of cleavage or skin showing. Because we live in this kind age, it is important that you steer clear of all things that force you to evoke the thoughts of self-comparisons.

Un-friending your ex keeps the breakup off your mind while preventing unfair comparisons. Most important it keeps the two of you from airing out everything that took place in your relationship – the good, the bad, and the ugly. This is a must because things that happen online can impact other areas of your life such as your career. There are increasing cases where people are laid off from their jobs or denied employment because of their behavior on social media. You do not want your career to be negatively impacted by things you may say during an emotional time.

Now it is time to take a bold step. Take a break from social media for thirty days.

Yes. No twitter, no Facebook, no Pinterest, no social media for thirty full days.

This is a very bold step that may at first sound stupid, but it is one, which has a whole range of personal and psychological benefits. Because it is a habit that has been cultivated over a long period of time, there will be withdrawal after effects. It may seem easy at first by logging off on your computer and removing the application(s) from your mobile device but the real test of endurance starts the second day when you impulsively reach out to check your latest notifications.

A few things you can do to fill the time typically spent on social media is engage in physical activities – they will keep your mind engaged and counter the feelings of withdrawal. You can also join a local group, go to the local festivals and start a new hobby. These activities have been known to be generally helpful. Stepping away for a while is very freeing. You'll find that you have more time, are able to focus on what matters, and you will gain a greater sense of clarity. During this time, focus on revisiting your goals.

Before and after your break from social media, do not post anything about your relationship. Leave your relationship status alone, do not post anything about the breakup, and do not discuss why you broke up, when you broke up or anything else related to the break up. The end of a relationship must stay between the two people involved and those two only. Of course, you will have to tell close friends and family eventually but involving third parties too soon can create drama. When people start buzzing over a breakup, drama is inevitable. Everyone has something to say and at least one person is bound to make a comment that irritates someone else. It is important to note that even though the thirty-day break is helpful; it also has its own downsides. You may be cut off from very important news that may be beneficial to you. You may also miss out on juicy news making the rounds while not being able to keep up with some engagements.

Nevertheless, every good thing comes at a cost. Let's say you wanted to lose ten pounds of body fat within a certain period of time. You go through painful measures such as sticking to low calorie meals, subjecting your body to intense exercises, all in order to reach the goals you set. Though your body may fight back in its desire to return to its default state, you endure the process and stick to your new regime. This reflects the reality that anything good must be fought for and it comes after giving up something else.

The above example is very similar to being heart-broken and going through the process of moving on. You must be ready to cut all ties to your ex-boy-friend for a period of time. Cutting all ties both in the physical world and in the social media world. Though you may fail in strictly sticking to the 30-day break from social media, you must keep at it. If you cannot go for 30 days straight, then break the period into smaller sections. A five-day break or a seven-day break may be enough to helping you cope with the withdrawal symptoms.

CHAPTER SIX
Turn a Painful Breakup into a Victory

A breakup can make you stronger than ever if handled correctly. Failed relationships come with a long list of lessons, experiences, and motivations. They force you to self-reflect in order to pick yourself up and brush yourself off successfully. As a result, you come back as a better, more experienced, independent, and mature woman with a lot to offer.

Everyone has different breakup styles but one thing you really want to do is express gratitude for the lessons learned. Taking this step will free you of any remaining anger and resentment because it turns the positivity switch on in your brain. Relationships teach you something whether that lesson is about yourself, life in general, or loving another person. There are a few ways to express your gratitude, but before you do, make a list of the lessons learned. You may have learned how to be a better person, a better partner, or how be more open.

As mentioned earlier having a relationship with your ex will not be possible immediately after the breakup. Once you are no longer emotionally attached to your ex, friendship may be possible. Many women want to gage if as soon as someone mentions being friends with their exes even though it happens often. Expressing that gratitude may bring your ex back in the form of a good friend (after there has been time to heal and recover). Think about this for a moment. You liked/loved your ex at one point, you know a lot about each other, you cared for them enough to build a relationship and connect on a romantic level, you shared good times, laughed, and shared interests so why is a friendship impossible? Some duos don't work romantically while a friendship is able to thrive and last a lifetime once romantic feelings drift away. The people you welcome into your life and those who earn a place in it are valuable so don't rule out the possibility of a friendship in the future.

Additionally, taking steps to express gratitude will boost your emotional maturity and put life into perspective. After you have a list of all the great things you gained from the relationship, choose how you would like to express your gratitude for them. Letter writing is a lost art well suited for releasing thoughts. Write a letter expressing gratitude for the good times and express how they made a difference in your life.

Finding light in a negative event reflects well on you and displays a healthy mindset. Staying hurt, angry and bitter does the opposite. Life is too short. All relationships have good times so highlight them and be thankful that you had them. If you are not ready to possibly open up communication with your ex because you fear a relapse, write the letter. Just don't send it yet. In time, you'll be ready.

The breakup makeover is real and you can pull it off like any A-lister. Being single again is a new chapter so welcome the newness by refreshing your hair and makeup. This is in no way intended to change how you look but rather enhance what you have going on and ensure your appearance matches your newfound outlook on life. A wardrobe and hair refresh also gives you an excuse to be creative and have a little fun.

For the wardrobe, begin with what you already have. Set aside a Saturday to go through your closet. Most of us have items that still have tags that have been hanging out in the back of the closet for months. Pull those out, take a look, try on the items and keep the pieces that work. Items that don't should be set aside to sell or donate. Once you know what you are keeping, rework what you have. After you've had fun with that, plan a day of shopping and really treat yourself. Buy pieces that you feel nothing less than amazing in and don't be afraid to step away from what you would normally wear. You've evolved so evolve your fashion as well. Classic silhouettes, form fitting, bright colors, prints and deep, mysterious hues are all great choices.

As for hair, try a new style that compliments your face shape or update your current one. The person to consult for this would obviously be your hair stylist. They often have great recommendations for their clients. Even if your hair is fab and you love it, change it up a bit. What you don't want to do, however, is make a drastic change that you will have to deal with for months. Refreshing changes are good while drastic changes are often made on impulse, meaning you'll regret it later. To keep your decision-making on the right path, make changes that enhance what already makes you a stunner. If your budget allows, also treat yourself to a spa day or at least a massage.

Feeling lousy post breakup is normal but moping will only worsen the negative emotions. Staying in a negative mindset often leads to feeling pathetic and then things just go downhill from there. Get up and do something! Do anything outside of your normal routine. You have experienced a big change so welcome that and use it in your favor. Cook a meal you have never tried before, take a spur of the moment weekend trip with your bestie, dedicate more time to big picture stuff, or try waking up a little earlier in the morning before work to start your day doing something you want to do. Whatever you do, make sure it is productive and benefits your mind, body, and/or spirit. Even better, make it a point to step out of your comfort zone. Snapping yourself out of breakup mode with newness is extremely effective. In fact, newness is going to make you look at your life in a whole new light. At this point, life should be improving with each passing day. Freshness is the way to get excited for what's to come.

Although they shouldn't, relationships hold us back to an extent. Perhaps your ex managed to talk you out of certain goals you wanted to accomplish so the two of you could spend more time together or relationship turmoil hindered your ability to be productive. You are free and your free time belongs to you and you only. This means you do what you want, when you want, and how you want, without anyone's input. First, take care of the important stuff you've wanted to accomplish. This can be a project around the house, devoting time to friendships you have neglected, visiting parents, siblings or that volunteer work you have been putting off for months. Catch up on things you want to do for entertainment like taking up a new hobby or anything you couldn't get your ex to do with you. This is the time to be selfish. Live it up!

Once you are able to celebrate, it is safe to say that you navigated your way through the breakup. At the start, you may have doubted that you would make it through. Doubt is part of the process, however, everyone has the ability to heal and overcome. Is it easy? No. Will you be an emotional mess at some point? Sure. Luckily, pain and sadness are only temporary.

CHAPTER SEVEN
Breaking Free After your Breakup

Asoul tie is a link between two people on a spiritual and/or emotional level. It encompasses the heart, mind, emotions, passions and desires. This tie is either a result of an intense emotional/spiritual association or comes after physical intimacy. A soul tie established before physical intimacy and is often very deep and true – it's a connection many of us dream of having with a partner. When two souls essentially become one, an advanced level of love and understanding is achieved. This soul tie creates a bond in which you can just be with each other without saying a word or know what one another is thinking with a quick glance. Although not exclusive to marriage, this type (often referred to as a godly soul tie) positively impacts relationships and helps them survive the test of time.

The other is associated with "ungodly relationships" or those of a physical nature. You know, that strong emotional pull felt towards a person you connected with physically. No matter which one you are facing, breaking free can present a challenge and come with emotional turmoil when the relationship ends. Let's discuss how soul ties are formed in depth.

Close relationships result in soul ties. There are instances in which you meet someone, a relationship steadily evolves and something just clicks. This is often a romance but can also happen in friendships. The more you learn about each other, the more your souls become intertwined. This results in a form of emotional dependence. One does not feel whole without the other and cannot imagine not having that person in their life. This can be a healthy dynamic driven by love and care or an unhealthy one. The quality of the relationship directly impacts the soul tie. Bad relationships result in bad soul ties while good relationships result in good soul ties.

Whether we like it or not, sex comes with some strings attached. Sharing such an intimate moment (or a series of moments) with a person establishes a connection. It is like gluing two pieces of paper together. When paper is glued and then pulled apart, much like casual sex, pieces of glued paper remain, meaning a piece of that partner stays with you. Becoming "one flesh" without the mental connection and commitment often results in damaging heartbreak. Despite feeling true in the moment, soul ties formed this way lack depth.

Commitments and marriage vows are an obvious way soul ties are formed. Entering a monogamous relationship or exchanging vows in a marriage ceremony signifies becoming one with your partner. This makes it more challenging to break free if the relationship ends.

Soul ties are great in theory. Intertwining one soul with another is something special WHEN that relationship is healthy. With a healthy soul tie comes fulfillment, happiness, new experiences and so much more. Such a bond gives two people the capacity to build a romance that grows with each passing year. On the other hand, they can significantly hinder us. Whether it's unhealthy from the start or becomes unhealthy following a breakup, they can negatively impact people. Breakups are processed as traumatic events and when soul ties remain, a person experiences something best described as a scattered soul. They go about their life, but fail to make a clean break. For example, those whose soul is scattered may try dating others but bring their ex (or exes) into conversations. They may also cyber stalk during their free time and continually vent about the relationship to friends/family.

If a connection with a partner leaves you confused and you don't know where you stand, that shows an unhealthy dynamic. Perhaps feelings are one sided or, you know that continually pining for this person is not what you need in your life. When the heart and mind are sending different messages, confusion sets in and a point is reached when you don't know why you feel the way you do or are behaving in such a way.

Persisting with something we know is wrong makes us uneasy. This uneasiness comes in the form of anxiety, exhaustion, and sadness. That is why unhealthy soul ties weigh so heavy on us. The bond created by unhealthy soul ties is hard to let go of; even though we know we must in order to be happy, healthy, and whole.

Put things into perspective for a moment. Is lust or physical desire a foundation worthy of a soul tie? No, of course not. Yeah, having such a connection with a partner is fun, exciting and gratifying in the moment but does it contribute anything else to your life? No. Again, having such an unhealthy dynamic from the start is no way to develop something meaningful. The worst part is, that type of connection fizzles over time and leaves you wondering, "What was I thinking?"

Whether overbearing or controlling behavior is from you or a partner, there's no place for it in a relationship. A bond is just that, not a power struggle.

Passive tendencies

Relationships worth having are ones that you are free to share your thoughts, ideas, and viewpoints. A partner that is either passive or sparks your passive tendencies indicates an imbalance in the relationship. There may be a connection but a level of comfort and openness is missing. Without that, an intertwining of souls (in a healthy way) is almost impossible.

Breaking soul ties is a tough task but once a relationship is over, it is time to start taking the necessary steps. Here they are below.

ACKNOWLEDGE AND REFLECT

To break a soul tie, you first must acknowledge that there is a problem. The best way to do that is reflecting. Reflection helps you realize when a pull towards someone is becoming a hindrance. Once a breakup takes place, the relationship is over. Rather than staying in limbo for an extended period and wasting precious moments of your life, decide to start moving forward to free yourself.

CONFESS

There are many ways to confess or acknowledge how this soul tie has negatively impacted you. You can talk to family, a close friend, anonymously blog about it or take a more spiritual/religious approach if you wish. The point is expressing where you went wrong. When you do, something clicks, making you less likely to repeat that mistake. As you know, you need to release those ill feelings to break free from the things holding you back. That is what this step is about. Additionally, it kick starts the next step – accountability.

Hold Yourself Accountable

No matter what led to the breakup, hold yourself accountable for the part you played. A soul tie has two ropes and one of those ropes is yours so take responsibly for any wrongdoing. If the relationship was all wrong from the start, accept that. Were the signs of an unhealthy tie there all along? Hold yourself accountable for ignoring them. Identifying what you did wrong helps break soul ties for good.

Forgive

Breaking a tie and moving on also requires forgiveness. This requires forgiving both yourself and your ex. No matter what happened, there was a time when you connected on a positive level so even though the situation wasn't right for you, forgive and put it in the past. Also, remember that holding onto that anger continues to feed the negativity. Who wants that?

Break and Remove

Lastly, make a clean break and remove yourself from the soul tie entirely. Just remember that an all-encompassing connection does not fade immediately but it will in time. To help with the process, get rid of any gifts, mementos or anything else that reminds you of your former partner. The "out of sight, out of mind" approach is quite helpful.

Overall, soul ties are powerful and often deep but breaking free after a breakup is possible. You can overcome the obstacles and come out a better person in the end. The key to success is having an understanding that ties are binding but fragile and you commit to taking the necessary steps to move on with your life.

CHAPTER EIGHT
Know When You're Ready
to the Dating Scene

It is difficult to decipher when you're ready to start dating again. Breakups are tough and knowing when to make your return is all about timing. Return too soon and you are destined for more heartbreak. As for those who wait too long, well, you're depriving yourself of something new and exciting. Ideally, you don't want to join either group so you must listen to your heart and mind. Here's how to determine when you're ready.

Dating before you are ready is both wrong for you and whomever you decide to see. It is wrong for you because dating too early masks unresolved feelings and keeps them unresolved. Because of the lack of a resolution, you never truly move on because

65

there are no proactive steps being taken to change anything. This often leads to entering another relationship, although your heart isn't really in it, and the other person ends up hurt once they realize they were merely a distraction. As a result, you may end up in a worse position than you when you started.

Instead, you need time to heal. Go through all the stages of a breakup during this time, determine why it didn't work out, how you can improve as a partner, what was good and bad about the relationship AND get to know yourself again. Get to know the new you-the single you. Successfully navigating the many stages of a breakup should eventually end in having neutral feelings towards your ex.

For those unsure of what neutral feelings towards an ex feel like, it is reaching a point of peace and closure. You know, a healthy place. Upon reaching this point, you know it's over. Better yet, you have accepted the split and no longer feel an emotional pull towards him. Also, remember that neutral feelings often involve having love for your ex. You are happy to have been in the relationship, still like him as a person, and may even remain part of each other's lives. You are just not in love anymore.

After you're over your ex, a reinvention of yourself completes the healing process. Although we hate to admit it, relationships change us and sometimes we lose sight of who we are. It is just so easy to be encompassed by the romance and love that nothing else seems to matter. When the romantic bond dissipates, most of us want to reinvent ourselves but quite often this "reinvention" is going back to the person we were. We just don't realize it. When in a relationship we get comfortable and put less effort into our appearance. When single again, we want to look our best, feel attractive, get the mind straight and regain the confidence needed to get out there and meet prospective dates.

Coming into your own, positively impacts self-confidence by helping you discover who you are without a man. You're only ready to date when your self-confidence is intact and strong. As you know, connecting with someone new requires a good sense of self. Otherwise, you're just presenting a shell of yourself.

You've Thought About What You Want, What You Don't and Have Identified Deal Breakers

This is a biggie that is often overlooked. Before returning to the dating scene, you must know what you want, what you don't, and the things you will not tolerate. When deciding what you want in a partner, be honest with yourself and go way deeper than physical appearance. Consider the traits you find irresistible, what energy you are looking for in a partner, the qualities required for things to work long term and list some qualities that best compliment you. After going over the good, reflect on what you don't want in a partner. Look back at past relationships; pinpoint the things that didn't sit right with you and the poor choices you made in terms of partner selection.

Now let's talk deal breakers. Deal breakers go beyond what you don't want in a partner. They are things you cannot stand. You can also take into consideration hygiene (body odor, cleanliness), negative personality traits (arrogance, controlling tendencies, an overwhelming heir of dishonesty), social habits and dating behaviors (having multiple partners). This list develops with experience so take a mental visit of past relationships to identify your non-negotiables.

If you need help organizing your thoughts, make a list or take a more artistic approach with a vision board. This may seem a bit extra for some but knowing what you truly want and what's best for you is important. Otherwise, you're dating with no direction, which increases the chance of repeating unsuccessful dating patterns. Organized thoughts and a clear direction mean you're ready.

You know how you close yourself off from newness after a breakup? The want to do your own thing is too strong, while the desire to gain new experiences is nonexistent. This phase is normal. It is comfortable and needed after a relationship ends. Once this changes and the urge to get back out there and experience life returns, make your return to the dating scene. But first, step out of your comfort zone and try new things. It doesn't have to be anything drastic, just new. Travel to a destination you have always wanted to visit, go on that crazy adventure with your bestie that you've been talking about for months or learn a new skill. After that, start addressing your love life. Introduce yourself to some attractive guys when out with friends, engage in conversation, exchange numbers and get drinks, coffee, or dinner with a few you're interested in. Just keep things fun and lighthearted.

Also, be sure to carry your desire for new experiences over into your love life. For example, online dating may be something you've wanted to try, perhaps speed dating recently sparked your interest or date someone that is not your "type" and see what happens. It makes no sense but sometimes you don't know what you want until you spend a few hours with it.

Lastly, remember that connecting with new romantic interests brings new experiences. They may invite you to do something or go somewhere you have not been or introduce you to a new hobby/interest. No matter what new experience you gain, enjoy and know that your openness means you're ready to date.

The final sign that you are ready to start dating again is an excitement and drive to meet new people. This is usually lost after a breakup. You want to stay in a bubble, keep your friends/family close and exclude everyone else. However, when you're over your ex that bubble gets boring and you burst out. Before you know it, you're looking for excuses to talk to new people whether they are a prospective date or simply someone to socialize with. The reason for this is loneliness. Although you have your inner circle and have gotten over the breakup, a void remains. Not only are you missing that partnership but also you're probably a few friends short (people do take sides after a split). Because of this, you want to branch out and make a few casual friends. You know, the friends you call up when you want to have a fun night out.

Additionally, spark up a conversation with a cutie just for kicks or make it a point to go out on the weekends to mingle. In other words, when you're excited about meeting new people, go out and meet a few. When you do, put your best self forward by smiling and most importantly, be your true self.

If all these signs are there, it is time to start dating again! These are good indicators the heart is healed; you are feeling confident, self-assured, know what you want, are craving new experiences, and want to socialize. When you do start to date, don't forget to take full advantage of all that the single life has to offer. Embrace your freedom, get out there, and do not be afraid to date. Finally, take time before entering anything exclusive. As for those who are not ready, be patient with you. You'll know when the time is right.

NOTES

Tannan, D. (2007). *You Just Don't Understand* (1 edition (February 6, 2007) ed.). New York, New York: William Morrow Paperbacks.